C000005542

Endless thanks to the following ki

Ellie, Caitlin and Sophie of Poor Michelle for giving me the space to make the show happen.

Everyone who helped us debut the show in Edinburgh, especially Hannah Azuonye, Jon Matthews, Weibke Green and our friends at Feat. Theatre. A special shout out to Georgia Artus at Vintage Vibes.

Extra thanks to Jon for reading the script countless times and still being nice about it.

The extended Gauge family for their food/house/car/ emotional support throughout the process. Also my family for being wonderful and Nanny for being an inspirational woman.

Jamie Eastlake, Jo Langdon, Chris Haydon, Jethro Compton, Charlie Beaumont, Henry Shields, Gilly and Nigel Anderson and Michael Jinks.

Ben Giles for being roped in big time and not complaining.

And biggest thanks of all to Ellie Gauge who made *Violet* enjoyable from start to finish and whom I wish to make plays with forever.

Bebe Sanders

VIOLET

OBERON BOOKS
LONDON

WWW.OBERONBOOKS.COM

First published in 2019 by Oberon Books Ltd
521 Caledonian Road, London N7 9RH
Tel: +44 (0) 20 7607 3637 / Fax: +44 (0) 20 7607 3629
e-mail: info@oberonbooks.com
www.oberonbooks.com

A catalogue record for this book is available from the British Library.

PB ISBN: 9781786827180
E ISBN: 9781786827234

Cover design by Jethro Compton

Printed and bound by 4EDGE Limited, Hockley, Essex, UK.
eBook conversion by Lapiz Digital Services, India.

Visit www.oberonbooks.com to read more about all our books and to buy them. You
will also find features, author interviews and news of any author events, and you can
sign up for e-newsletters so that you're always first to hear about our new releases.

Printed on FSC accredited paper

10 9 8 7 6 5 4 3 2 1

Violet was first performed in August 2018 at Zoo Southside, Edinburgh with the following creative team:

Writer/ performer: Bebe Sanders

Director/producer/designer: Ellie Gauge

Production manager: Ben Giles

and at The Bunker Theatre, London in January 2019:

Writer/performer: Bebe Sanders

Director/producer/designer: Ellie Gauge

Production manager: Ben Giles

Sound designer: Julian Starr

Lighting designer: Ed Theakston

Characters

BERTIE
Female, late 20s.

Lines spoken by Violet should be spoken in a
Devonian/West Country accent.

[1]

A change is as good as a rest. That's what
they say, isn't it? A change, is as good as
a rest. But what they really mean is like, ← first change
a haircut. Or a new duvet cover. Or, I
dunno, a spin class.

Do you know how much a spin class ←
costs in London? Millions of pounds.
Seriously. Same with yoga. And as far as
I'm aware no one found enlightenment via
sexy, expensive activewear and Namaste
hashtags.

I tried early nights, I tried journaling my
feelings. I bought a notebook especially
FOR journaling my feelings. Has a peach
with a face on it saying 'Life is Peachy'.
But – it's not, is it? That's just Paperchase
doing marketing. It's just a lie. I tried a pot
plant. Genuinely – bought a pot plant and
put it next to my bed in the hope it was
physically going to remove the sadness
from my head whilst I slept through
photosynthesis or whatever. But also – if
I'm being totally honest – because it would
look good on Instagram if I ever took a

photo of my bed. Because maybe that's the answer. I tried eating kale, meditation apps, all of it. All of it costs money and none of it works.

And the truth is I don't have the energy, for any of it. I want to, but I just don't.

And you know, yeah, maybe this stuff works elsewhere, but in London, in London – everything is so much harder. It's like… sludge. It's thick and heavy and full of people struggling against each other, in order to try and get… something, and no one is managing it and it's hard and it's lonely and it's really, really expensive and… Just trying to do the day feels pointless and impossible.

And then I got fired. Literally just walked into the office one day and Karen tells me they're downsizing and won't be needing me anymore. Just like that – like, I'm sorry Karen, I'm aware that all I do is eat the staff biscuits and moan about you behind your back but that doesn't mean you can fire me. If I'm not an editorial assistant… Who am I?

And then – I mean it's like dominoes isn't it. So then I'm not working, well – I get a job in a bar, and I am such a waste of space, like, just this horrible ball of misery. I am twenty-seven years old – why am I working in a bar? So I'm coming back to my boyfriend Tommy at weird hours with a shitty negative attitude and clothes that smell like B.O. and beer, and so obviously he dumps me. I mean, it's fine. I was actually going to do it anyway, it's not a big deal he just got there before me but it does mean I have to move out of the flat I was sharing rent on – which then basically makes me homeless too, and...

Yeah, I could have moved in with my mum but I mean – her endless stream of boyfriends makes it abundantly clear that her priorities are very much elsewhere. The latest one walks around in harem pants with no shirt on and really, really needs to cut his toenails. Doesn't pay rent but spends all day cooking dahl in her kitchen and calls me "sweetheart". No thanks. I'd rather not be a part of that.

So… I've come down here. Because – sure. A change is as good as a rest, but actually – a rest sounds better.

Why here exactly? Couldn't tell you. I just needed to get away. I needed to feel like I could be somewhere where no one knew who I was.

Also my cousin is away for the summer so I could rent her flat. And by rent I mean live in. Without paying.

The house is very 'nice', it's – I mean, it's a bit… She's a fan of a shabby chic slogan wall decal. Put it that way.

"Sticky fingers, muddy paws, and hearts full of love"

It's sweet I guess. I mean Jesus – she's only three years older than me and has a mortgage, a kid, a husband and a John Lewis sofa, so who am I to judge her?

It's a five minute walk to the beach. A two minute walk to the town. There's a café, there's a supermarket. I am going to

4

have to get a job – so tomorrow I'll walk in and hand my CV out. Like a cretin. I'll probably end up behind a bar again wont I?

That feeling – that I was living in the wrong life – it was there. I just couldn't hear it over all the noise. It was like a mosquito in the room, the sound wasn't exactly loud, but it was there, and it was persistent, and it was becoming impossible to sleep through.

It's just that... now I'm here – it's like someone has switched that noise off. And the silence is utterly terrifying.

***

[2]

Well, Friday's here. And I've done nothing. Apart from sleep, watch 'Cash in the Attic', and cry. A lot. I still haven't made it into town to apply for jobs, and I've exclusively eaten white bread and an ancient packet of Parma Violets that I found at the bottom of my rucksack. It was only tonight, cocooned in a duvet with the blinds drawn, weeping into a pickle sandwich because cheese was too expensive I realised – I need to take a long hard look at myself. I need to wash, get a grip. I can't keep this up or it's going to get really ugly.

So tonight I've come down to the beach for a walk. It's the last thing I feel like doing but, I'm trying. I think, "oh maybe it'll be nice to walk barefoot" – healing power of nature and all that – but the sand is wet and poo-brown and when I walk it pushes through the gaps in my toes like an over-affectionate slug. It's overcast and – I just feel grey – like a dimmer light that someone has left on the lowest setting.

It starts drizzling then, and that sets me off crying again – because apparently I can't even time a walk, so I sit down on the wet sand and experience this darkness that I honestly think might physically suck me up and remove me from existence.

There is nothing for me in London. Nothing for me here. No ties, no job. No relationship. Mum would say something like "Oh darling, that's so freeing". But to me it just feels like no one would notice if I'm gone. And I know this is privileged pain. I know really I'm OK – that I'm safe, that compared to most people I am in the best position. That I have opportunities and advantages and headstarts. But for some reason knowing that makes it even worse.

When I stand up, I realise the beach has slowly become shrouded in this thick sea mist. And – I actually can't see where I'm going. It's straight out of a horror film. I'm trying my best not to freak out but I can't pretend I don't feel fairly certain someone is behind me with an axe. So, I start running and–

Forcefully collide with a woman holding a fishing rod. After a lot of swearing and apologies from both parties, I clock that she's fairly old. Not decrepit or anything, but like, definitely over seventy. Mid- to late-seventies, maybe. I don't know.

There's an awkward silence and a deeply uncomfortable amount of eye contact whilst she pierces bait onto the hook with bony, expert fingers. It's all very fucking sinister and surreal and– Why is this old woman down on the beach in the mist and the dark… isn't that like, a really weird thing to do? But then, she smiles, holds her hand out and says, "I'm Violet. Nice to meet you"

"Bertie" I say.

"I know, it's awful isn't it. My mother called me Roberta, because she takes drugs. So my choice of nicknames are limited – you know, 'Rob', 'Bert' – I think she wanted a boy. Anyway–"

Violet doesn't care. She's eighty and she's trying to fish.

I make my way home, and she smiles, and turns back to the sea, standing with her fishing rod like a gnome.

And I'm so wrapped up in how shit
everything is, that I don't think anything
else of it.

***

[3]

BERTIE stands looking up at the shop front, CV in hand.

We're ten days in. And slowly, I'm starting
to sort myself out – not fully, because I've
still got half a packet of Hovis soft slice and
I'm not one for waste, but – baby steps. I'm
trying to get some health and structure into
my life, and I'm starting with a job.

'Christine's cake parlour'. Do I want to
work here? Absolutely not.

"Hi there I was wondering if I could hand
in my CV. I'm new to the area…"

"Yes, yes I do have experience. With
cake…"

"Well Christine, who doesn't love a themed cupcake?"

"Really?"

"Well – he sounds mental – thank god he's your ex right?!… Thanks, yeah, well, if anything becomes available, my number's on the CV."

It's a light, early summer day. Cool enough to need a cardy but the sun's warm on my face and that's quite nice. There are boats, and seagulls and on the other side of the harbour amongst some trees, a little row of coloured houses that look like Lego.

I'm stood leaning against the harbour rail for a while, observing, trying to fathom why there are SO many topless male tourists with big, fat, swollen beer bellies, when she appears.

"Oh – hello"

She's come and stood right next to me, with a fishing rod again, and now we're in daylight I can get a proper look at her. One word. Crocs. She's got a lot of long white hair and it's piled up on top of her head in a kind of messy knot – her clothes look... organic, and she's tanned, and wrinkled, and on the collar of her dress is a little brooch.

"It's disgusting isn't it–"

I follow her gaze and realise she's talking about the man with the belly on the beach,

"I mean, why is it glistening like that?"

"Well," I say, "maybe he's oiled it up. Lubrication for the occasion."

We stand like that for a while and– everyone just talks to you down here, it's bizarre. I tell her I'm down from London for the summer, and that today I am looking for work.

"Work?" she says. "Well – in that case... perhaps... you'd like to come for some dinner? I might be able to help you? Look – I'm up there."

And she points to a big old house perched
on the cliff at the far end of the beach.

"Come and have some supper. Tonight if
you like – 7 o clock?"

In the end I say yes. Bit weird.

***

[4]

Why am I here? I've arrived at seven like
she said, and – I think I have the right
place – but I mean, all I've got to go on
is the memory of her just pointing to a
random house and now I'm here. Why? I
know nothing about this woman. And I'm
stood outside her house on the doorstep
with a bunch of flowers like a twat.

I stay like that for seven minutes trying to
pluck up the courage to ring the doorbell
when she walks past the kitchen window
and sees me anyway – she's in a sort of
kimono type thing that I think must be
a dressing gown and I think, "Oh Christ

she's forgotten" but turns out she hadn't at all. It's just a bit of an eccentric choice of outfit. She spent a lot of time in Japan in her youth, apparently.

"I expect you're looking for my knocker" she says, as she opens the door.

I hand over my gift. I'd spent an hour in the Co-op beforehand trying to work out what to bring with me. What do you take to dinner with a pensioner? And a pensioner that you don't know. At all. I opted for a shit bunch of tulips in the end. I would've bought a bottle of wine but I didn't know if she drank. Turns out I really needn't have worried about that.

Actually, it turned out to be quite a nice evening. She poured me a glass of wine and pottered around the kitchen cooking, waving a spatula around quite flamboyantly and flicking bits of fish all over the place. And, looking around the house I'm kind of surprised. There's so much going on. Artwork and photographs and books and... colour. Like – a life that is still happening. I don't know what I was expecting but it wasn't this.

And she's chatting away, the whole time, like she's known me for years. Which she hasn't. I don't really understand why she's being so… kind.

When she asks where I'm at in my life, I don't give her the full story, no one needs that. But, I do tell her that I don't really have a plan.

She smiles and tells me that I have the world at my fingertips.

Now – I know she's only being friendly but this is an expression that really gets on my tits. You only ever hear old people saying it, don't you? You don't hear someone your own age going "Oh don't worry about being heartbroken and skint mate – you've got the world at your fingertips!" And what does it mean? I feel like I've got the world stuck up my arse hole.

I was going to say as much but… You know, wrong crowd.

After dinner, and what I think was her –
sixth? – glass of wine, she pushed her plate
to one side and said,

"Right Bertie. I like you. Twelve pounds
an hour. Full-time. I'll feed you. It'll be
some organising, a bit of clearing out… I
might start needing a bit of help with– well,
you can think of it as a sort of personal
assistant role. I need an open mind and a
can-do attitude – are you in? You can start
tomorrow"

I was trashed by this point. So by the looks
of things I said yes again.

***

[5]

Oh my God this was not the plan. All I
did was say yes to some dinner with an old
lady and now I'm apparently in full-time
employment. I'm supposed to be having a
break. This time last week I was sat in three
day old pants re-watching season three of
Love Island and it's all changed very fast.

She's working me like a goddamn dog;
filing, and sorting and organising.

Obviously on the first day I arrived late,
with a hangover I genuinely thought
might end me. I don't know how she was
seriously expecting to see me at 9am. Why
does drunk Bertie say yes to everything?
She's such a fucking idiot. When I did
eventually turn up Violet was waiting at the
door and said, "Nice of you to show up.
Get lost did you?", so that set a fairly clear
tone for the rest of the week.

I actually think the house is pretty cool. It's
cluttered, loads of stuff everywhere – lists
taped to practically every surface. But – it's
one of those places that makes me want to
poke about, you know? Be nosy.

There's paintings on all the walls, some
she's done herself, she told me. She has a
collection of rubber ducks in the bathroom
– hers, apparently. She doesn't have
grandkids. I asked.

She doesn't really talk about family at all,
actually.

Ummm… She's cooked for me every day
I've been here. Eggs, usually, for breakfast.
Haven't had a shit in days. Fish – I think
she goes out every day. Which is pretty
cool really. And the last couple of days
I've stayed for dinner too. Might as well.
Everyone loves a free meal right?

This particular afternoon, we're sat on
the floor in the brown-carpeted sitting
room, going through boxes and boxes
of paperwork. We're having a bonfire
on Friday night apparently. I'm sorting
through bills and boring subscription letters
when I come across a folder, sealed up
with more parcel tape than I'd ever seen in
my life.

"Jesus Christ Violet what have you got in
here?"

"Ooh I don't know" she says.

I manage to rip it open and a pile of
photographs spill out onto the floor in front
of me.

"Oh dear–" she says, "You weren't supposed to see *them*."

"Who WAS supposed to see them?!"

I spread them out and it's just, hundreds of black and white photographs, and there's a naked woman in every single one. We're talking 1930s naked though – like – really fucking classy.

"Violet, is this you?!"

She looks at them for a while, flicking through casually. Occasionally going, "oh yes" or, "oh dear" depending on the angle, and then she stands up, like she's going to make a speech. Which she basically does.

"They say that when you're naked you're vulnerable don't they? But I've always thought a woman's body to be a very powerful thing, really. Do you know, I used to daydream about how the horrible man who owned my flat on Kenton Street would react if I were to open the door to him with no clothes on. Marvellous. I think my body was, is, rather marvellous. So yes, you will probably come across quite a few nudes. Most of them I took myself. Some of the more sexual ones were taken by lovers, but for goodness sake don't ask me who, I can't remember any of them. Tea?"

And off she goes out into the kitchen to make a pot of tea and find a packet of garibaldi.

Mic drop. BERTIE's jaw is wide open.

My new boss is an absolute badass.

***

[6]

I don't want to curse anything, but I've started to feel alright coming in to work each day. When I wake up in the morning now, I don't immediately feel... despair.

It's easy to forget that a conversation, basically, is just two people trying to connect. There's a lot of bullshit, isn't there? I don't think I'd noticed that before.

There's no bullshit with Violet. She'll say something blunt like "Life can be lonely" And I'll be like "Yeah it can" and that's it. Then we'll just crack on. It's nice.

I take the cliff path to her house every morning. It's a longer route, but it's nicer. That's what she said to me – "Bertie, take the cliff path, it's nicer." And I'd gone "Yeah but it's longer." And she said, "But it's nicer." And – she was right. It is nicer. It's a really lush way to start the day, especially when the suns shining like this. It makes me feel very 'present'. Not a feeling I've been familiar with before. Like there's room to just… be a person on the planet. Maybe this is what I could have achieved through £25 yoga classes. And yeah – my mood is surprising me a bit. I mean don't get me wrong, I know there's still the problem of, well, 'my entire life' somewhere…

But it's quiet at the moment. It's not screaming at me. It's just following me like a bit of an annoying friend. A bit like Donkey in 'Shrek'. Like, yeah it's there,

and it's annoying. But we can deal with
Donkey.

This morning, when I arrive. She isn't
there. All the logs and bits of wood I've
collected over the week are stacked up
where I left them ready for the bonfire
tonight. I try knocking, and knocking
again, and waiting, but nothing. So – I try
the door, and it's unlocked.

"Violet?"

There is nothing.

It's a bit strange, but I assume that she
must have just popped out and I've maybe
just missed her. She must have left the
door open for me. Why else would it be
unlocked? I check the kitchen for a note,
but there isn't one, so I faff about with a
piece of toast and some coffee, notice she's
popped a couple of the naked photos on
the fridge, and after half an hour with still
no sign of her, I decide to just carry on
with the work we were doing yesterday. So
I make my way into the sitting room. It's
stuffy in there today. The curtains haven't

been drawn. It's all amber and hot and smells like carpet.

It's a weird feeling, being in someone's house without them. Everything kind of... stands out more.

I very slowly pull open the drawer on the side table.

Now, I have to say, in my defence, I do feel guilty – but, I justify it to myself by thinking that we'll probably go through all of this together anyway, so I'm not *really* doing anything out of line.

And it's well boring anyway. Two batteries, a funeral... pamphlet? What are they called? Flyers? A funeral programme?

Handful of nails, clothes brush and... ew, a gross mouldy banana. Really Violet?!

I go to slide the drawer back but it gets stuck on something that's slipped down and got wedged behind it, so, I put my hand in and pull it out.

It's an album, a kind of scrapbook. It's
got this brown leather cover and it's so
old that the pages are barely attached
and the binding has gone to shit. This
is more like it! Why is stuff like this so
exciting... I open it up, and a whole life
leaps up at me. It's a baby book. A record
of a little life. Handprints, mummy and
baby, a photograph of what I assume is
a much younger Violet holding this fat,
ruddy-looking baby boy. A lock of hair, a
letter from the tooth fairy – "We are sorry
to inform you, that the tooth fairy was
unable to leave funds this time, as you are
still sucking your thumb." Then pages of
first days at school, a mother's day card,
splashes of paint, and then... Nothing. The
rest of the book is empty.

Classic. Typical. Tell me one human being
that has ever finished a scrapbook. Why
are we so incapable of seeing these projects
through? Example, when my friend Sarah
had a baby, I decided I was going to knit
a jumper with ears on the hood for it. Her.

She's three now and I've still got a bag of purple wool in my wardrobe.

***

How I didn't hear her come in I have no idea.

"Oh shit – Violet! You scared me. Sorry. Um… I was just. Wait, where have you been?"

Turns out she'd forgotten. She'd forgotten I was coming. Which did strike me as really odd, because I'd been there every day for weeks now and … we had a whole routine and–

"Well then why was the door open?"

She's staring blankly at the book still in my hands. "Just stick it on the bonfire later."

"Um… OK. Why?"

"Some things are better forgotten" she says, and walks out of the room.

What is wrong with me? Why don't I
have any self-control? Why didn't I just
put it back? Or even better just not go
rummaging through her private property in
the first place? And also–

Why was the door unlocked?

***

[8]

She barely speaks a word to me after
that. I spend the whole afternoon setting
up the bonfire, trying to keep as busy as
I can, and every now and then she pops
out to chuck on a few cardboard boxes,
or crap from the shed. "We'd better wait
until it's dark before we light it" she says.
And – I overcompensate in a big way with
cheeriness like "OK great! Really good
idea. Should be great – perfect weather for
it. Really looking forward to it."

When it gets to about seven she shuffles
out and says, "Right." I throw a match
onto the pile and we sit around it together

in silence. Seems a bit extreme. I mean,
I get that she's annoyed at trespassing or
whatever, but the silent treatment? Seems
a bit harsh. I watch her as she takes the
book, and places it into the flames without
a word. Without a facial expression or
a flinch. Its pages curl up at the corners
and then fan out. And then, after a while
I realise the worst thing – she's crying.
She's illuminated by the fire and I can
see streams of tears washing down her
expressionless, old lady face… And then it
clicks. I am so stupid.

"Violet –"

"Go home now Bertie."

I don't know what to do. I grab a stick and
try to flick it out of the fire but it's too late

It just crumbles into ash. I am officially the worst person in the world.

***

[9]

That night, I can't sleep. Of course I can't. Knowing you're in the wrong is the worst feeling, isn't it? It's not like thinking 'Oh maybe I've done something wrong'. It's not 'the fear' after a night of drinking. Really knowing you've done something wrong, that you've hurt someone – it's like pain.

At 4am, I turn the light on. I get my phone. I do what anyone would do in this situation. I turn to Google.

BERTIE Googles

"How to make an old lady happy…"

Little tip – never, ever google 'how to make an old lady' happy at 4am unless you never want to sleep again. The world, the internet, is a dark, dark place.

'How to make an elderly citizen' – is that right? Is there a PC way of saying old person!? 'How to cheer up an old person.' 'How to brighten an elderly woman's day.'

After hours of trying to find the right wording, I finally come across something I think might work. An activity. It's of her era, it's 'physical, mood-lifting fun and a great way to make new friends, keep fit, and find like-minded people'– and the best bit – it has a 'try me' class for £5. I book it there and then, for next Friday. One week's time.

Darkness and fatigue can make us act in peculiar ways. But, it's booked. It's happening.

I am taking her to a Lindy Hop class.

***

[9]

'Get Happy' by Judy Garland plays and Bertie attempts to keep up with the routine.

***

[10]

Yeah I'll be honest, I've surprised myself.
She's glowing. I've had my first exercise
in months. Bloody yogis and exercise
do-gooders were right weren't they – it
really does make you feel better. Bastards. I
cannot feel my feet and I feel like I've been
punched in the abdomen but at this point,
I'm OK with that. We're all giggly and
high and excitable when we come out. It's
amazing. I really don't want the day to end,
so I suggest we go and get fish and chips.

"Ooh fantastic idea!" she says. She looks at me and her little blue eyes are sparkling. She's quite striking, really.

In the chip shop, I tell her I'll have a "small cod and chips please and um… also – could I have a pickled egg? please."

The woman at the counter pulls a face. Violet beams. "Two cod and chips and *two* pickled eggs please." She says to the woman. "Hugely underrated side dish. Shall we eat them on the beach?"

We walk out of the chip shop arm in arm like a couple of reprobates and I am the happiest I have been in months.

***

She wolfed them down quick enough. Jesus Christ.

"Work up an appetite in there did you?" She laughs at me and says, "Ooh I feel like I could do anything! Are we going to go again next week?"

And that makes my tummy flip and the good feeling vanishes instantly. I always knew I'd have to go but the thought of returning to London now makes me feel sick.

"I can't Violet. You know I have to go back to London next week. Victoria's coming back, needs the house. Remember? We talked about it…?"

We sit for a few minutes in silence and just, listen to the waves. There's something about the beach isn't there? Must be something about being on the edge… the end. As far as you can go.

"You could always stay with me?" she says.

Again, bit weird. Why? Why is she so desperate for me to stay? Like, Violet – why are you so obsessed with me?

No but seriously – I have a real problem in that I trust people far too easily and so far it's only ever got me into trouble. I should start learning from my mistakes. Tommy – trouble. Mum – trouble. That man on

Oxford street who asked to borrow my phone – trouble.

But then – I don't feel unsafe. My instincts aren't alerting me of any danger. But then my instincts haven't really resumed usual service yet, so I probably shouldn't trust them either. Last night I literally sat up in bed and realised I could push a hairgrip into my eye socket and nothing told me to stop, so…

Could I stay? I mean, I am going to have to go back at some point. I can't just… abandon my real life and take up residence with an eighty-year-old… I've still got stuff at Tommy's that I need to collect and it's all sort of on hold up there. There are ends to tie up. Projects to complete. You know.

But then, isn't there something quite nice about coasting? About not – finishing it all? And I really like it down here. You can get a pint for two quid. TWO QUID. And you know what, actually Christine's lavender cupcakes are second to none. Sure, I'm running away from a few problems. But maybe... maybe that's ok?

***

[11]

The next few months, I have to say, are flipping great. I'm totally in this bubble of life by the seaside and just enjoying myself and not thinking about anything. We are Fred *(she points to Violet)* and Ginger *(she points to her head)*. We go to Lindy Hop every week, she's obsessed. I'm fairly certain a lot of that is to do with the very attractive teacher, but, whatever it takes.

Around week three she started making comments to me like,

"He'd be a nice young man for you Bertie. Replace that nasty Tommy boy."

and, when I told her to calm down, I wasn't ready for anything yet, she said,

"What, not even a shag? Jesus, come on, I can't do it can I? You could at least take one for the team."

He's a good sport actually. He has a real soft spot for her. And to be honest I can understand why.

She walks in to the class and just kind of, lifts it. Everyone chats to her, she's interested in everyone. Makes everyone feel special. I don't even really know how she does it. It's this way of just... listening. I think we could all learn a lot from that. To listen more.

In week four, she farted in the middle of learning a Texas Tommy. Just, let it rip. Outrageously loud. Everybody stopped. The room went dead. Time and space stood still. And all she had to say for herself was, "Oh did everybody hear that?" Brilliant.

Then, a couple of weeks ago, something a bit strange happened. She was probably just tired, but, she snapped. We were learning this new step, and, yeah, to be fair, he was going pretty quickly. But, she turned really quite nasty on poor old Franc. Franc who up until this point couldn't do anything wrong.

"Slow the fuck down Franc! How am I supposed to learn that? You're going too bloody quickly! No respect."

The whole class was really taken aback, and he apologised, and did it again, but she wouldn't stop.

"Too fast! I can't learn it like that can I? So selfish. Stupid man."

In the end I had to take her home early. She was silent in the car, and then the next day back to normal. It was horrible. Really weird, and horrible.

Every week after the class, we stop off at the chippy and have fish and chips and a pickled egg, and undo any of the good the dancing would have done. But it's always my favourite part of the week, that. And the time when we talk. Properly talk.

We were sat like this the week she told me about her little boy.

"I love the sea" I'd said, "don't you?" And she raised her eyebrows and popped a chip into her mouth.

"We were on the beach" she'd said. "Just a normal afternoon, it was supposed to be. Sandcastles, paddling, rock pooling. You know how it is. But the tides can be so dangerous here Bertie. It looks peaceful and tranquil but it's raging underneath. He was so little. By the time I started looking for him it was too late".

She popped another chip into her mouth and that was that. I didn't feel like I needed to say anything. Just listened. We just, finished eating in silence and looked out

at the sea. Calm and peaceful – but raging
underneath.

***

[12]

I'm not proud of losing my temper. In fact,
I'm ashamed. But I was stressed, and she
was driving me up the wall. All day she'd
been faffing about. Decisions were taking
twice as long to make, everything was so
slow. And my life was starting to catch
up with me, turns out you can run away
from your problems – but you will just
run straight into brand new ones coming
from the opposite direction. I'd been living
with her for a while now, and slowly over
the months I'd started to get texts from
Tommy, saying things like "you know –
I'm totally happy to hold on to this stuff
but it is starting to get in the way." And
"hey just checking you got my last message
– really need this stuff moving", and phone
calls from my mother, in tears – "I just
don't know what it is with me and men!"
I could probably have a pretty accurate

guess Mum, my phone contract is about to run out, I need to renew the permit for the car in London before I'm charged a million pounds, Uncle Derek has started drinking again and would I mind calling cousin Amy because she's very upset. And it all climaxed when my old boss called me yesterday. We were in the kitchen. I was distracted anyway because Violet was shuffling about opening different drawers and moving stuff rather than just getting ready like I'd asked. We needed to leave for Lindy Hop at six and it was five to.

"Hi Karen. Yes, yes no I can chat – why? Oh... um, well, I've been away for a bit. No, um. Permanent, not necessarily – why? Right. Starting when? How much?! Yes, potentially, leave it with me, I have a few things to think over before I can just... by Monday? Right. Yes of course. Thanks Karen. I will. Bye."

When I hang up, Violet's stood with her top halfway over her head. "Violet what are you doing?"

She tells me she's getting changed.

'But you're already in your class outfit. Stop it." And I tug it down her body, her arm gets caught and she screams, totally over the top.

"What the fuck is wrong with you?! Stop it! Why are you screaming?!"

I know I'm being awful but I'm wound up. I go to get the keys from the hook in the hope that it might prompt her to get out of the door, now that we're running late. But they're not there.

"Violet, where are your car keys?"

She looks up at me blankly and – I just cannot figure out what's going on with her. It's like… there's only half of her.

"Violet? WHERE ARE YOUR KEYS?"

"You've probably taken them" she says. And that's it –

"Why the fuck would I have taken them Violet? Why? Why would I do that? Why would I hide a set of keys, from myself?

Obviously I didn't do that did I? I left them on the hook, right here. So unless we find them in the next two minutes, we're not going!"

"You've taken them" she says again.

"WELL THEN I GUESS WE'RE NOT FUCKING GOING ARE WE?"

***

[13]

I'm feeling good about this decision. This is good. Going up to London for the weekend, suss out the new job offer, quick sweep up of everything. Tie up all my loose ends in one go. Collect my stuff from Tommy, move the car, see my mother. I'm going to finish all of the projects. I am essentially Superwoman. I'm sat on the train and I'm watching the world go by and – yeah, it's nice. Hello outside of the countryside. Real life. This is good. God, I've been so wrapped up in Violet. Still haven't found the car keys so had to get a

taxi to the station. I do feel maybe a tiny
bit guilty about the fact that I've just left a
note. She might be a bit pissed at that but–
I'm sure she can manage a weekend on
her own. She's fine. Course she is – she's
Violet. She's made of steel. The buffet
cart comes down the aisle and yeah, you
know what – I'm feeling wild, so I spend
three hundred pounds on a PG Tips and a
packet of shortbread. Nice. I take it off the
man but he's not put the lid on properly so
it slips off and spills scorching hot tea all
down my arm and into my lap. Fucksake.
Oh, sorry don't worry at all – no need for
an apology. Dickhead.

I step out into the station and – noise. The
noise. Turned back on. Very loud. Sirens.
Football crowds. Just – masses of people.
Fucking pigeons in my way and – now I
have shit on my suitcase and – why isn't
the wheel turning properly? Nope. I'll
just drag it. That's fine. It's old anyway.
Rummage for my ticket – jeans are still
damp. Man at barriers. Not an off peak
train. OK. Could you just – would you
mind just letting me through though?

Couldn't you just be a human being and just let me through?

No.

BERTIE takes a deep breath.

OK. An extra twenty quid on a new train ticket. It's fine. I've barely spent anything recently. Because – it's really cheap back at – oh my God I think my period has just started. No. Please not now. Please, please not now. Tie my hoody around my waist.

WHERE THE FUCK IS MY MOTHER? Try her phone. No answer. Of course there isn't. I doubt she's even got it on her. Half five we said. Half five at Paddington. That's definitely where I am. And it's definitely quarter to six. Supposed to be meeting Tommy at half past. Really, really don't want to go on my own. Try her three more times, no answer. Five to six. Drag my suitcase to the Underground.

On the Underground. Hot. So. So. Hot.

Arrive at Tommy's, sweating, voicemail from Mum – "Simon and I are just in the Lebanese sweetheart but I can still come and meet you if you like?" Mum? Fuck off. – Hi. Tommy. Ow my heart hearts.

"I'm really worried about you babe. You look tired." Just ignore it, pick up your boxes, and get out. "I really hope you're looking after yourself."

"Where's the bag of wool I left in the wardrobe? What do you mean you threw it away? Yes I know it had been there for years but it was mine and I was going to knit a jumper for Sarah's baby and now I can't because you've–"

Tommy kissing me. Don't want it. Yes I do. I'm a rubbish feminist. My heart hurts. My head can't– get out. Get to the car. Parking ticket. But I renewed it. I renewed it! Yes I would call the council but their office hours are impenetrable– and–

Missed call from Karen – "Can you come in on Tuesday instead? Totally bogged down – Susan's off sick so you might have

a bit of extra workload to start off with but
think it'll do you good and can you–"

NO.

NO NO NO NO NO. Fuck this. Fuck you
Tommy, fuck you Mum, fuck you Karen,
and anal parking ticket man and poorly
Susan and FUCK YOU LONDON!

Give me Lindy Hop, and pickled eggs, and
Violet over this any day.

I'm going home.

***

[14]

I breathe differently here. A breath of fresh
air – really… there's a different rhythm. A
different pace. Like time hasn't quite made
it down here. It's just going dark when I get
off the train. The sun has stained the sky
purple as it's slipped down behind the sea.
I don't know how long the walk from the

station takes me, but it's good. Cool, and quiet, and good.

When I get to the house, Violet is sat at the kitchen table with her glasses on a chain around her neck, reading. She looks up at me and–

***

Jesus I need to learn to hold my drink next to her. Eight gin and tonics. Eight. She's seventy-nine. It's not normal.

I get up woozily to go and have a wee. The familiarity of the house feels so good even after being away for such a short space of time. Like I want to hug the floorboards. Like stepping onto land after being on a boat. I sit on the loo without turning the light on, think maybe I'll try for a poo but, no, it's 4am, who am I kidding. So I flush. And just as I'm about to leave, I hear... jangling. From... the toilet. The flush, is jangling.

I lift off the ceramic lid of the cistern, plunge my hand into cold water, and pull out the car keys. The blood pulses, loud and fast in my ears. Just the same as it did when I realised Tommy had been sleeping with my best friend Sophie. It was a sock, that I found. Not a lipstick, or an earring, or anything romantic. Just an ugly old trainer sock. But it was enough. Funny, how one little item, a pair of keys, or a sock, can confirm something inside you that you didn't even realise you knew. Because, when you know something. You do know. You just do. You can waste as much time as you like trying to convince yourself, or others, or ignore it, or bend it or justify it any which way you like. But really, if you KNOW something. You should listen to it. Ignored knowings have an ugly habit of reappearing until they're listened to.

You can run from problem to problem and
get nowhere. I think the secret might be to
stop running.

***

[15]

The next day, I feel different. My first
thought isn't about me, for a start. She still
makes eggs, bless her, and every move
I analyse, trying to see if there are any
changes I can spot. She's slow, kind of...
mournful. "Are you OK this morning, Vi?"
She looks at me with milky, worried eyes.

So I take her hand in mine. It is so soft.
Like silk. Like Powder. I can feel the gentle
bones through the skin. It sounds silly but,
I feel maternal and comforted at the same
time. Like I can feel the wisdom of her
years behind us, and the empty possibility
of mine ahead.

"Why didn't you tell me Violet?" I ask.
"You don't need to be embarrassed"

"Oh please" she says. She sighs and stands up, "Shall I make some tea?"

I tell her she probably should. Not sure either of us can handle this chat without it.

BERTIE contemplates for a beat

Why, how, do I manage to make EVERYTHING about me? It's actually disgusting. It's a sickness. Here I am having a huge flap about everything, whilst she's just been getting on with… this. And now I'm trying to take on her problems too – as if she owes them to me. She has no obligation to tell me anything. She didn't tell me because she didn't want to. She owes me nothing.

''I won't have you staying here Bertie'' she says, as she sits back down with the tea. "It's not your job to stay and look after me. I don't want to be a burden. You accept this job and you go back to London."

But we are a team, me and her. We have shit to do. We have a commitment to a Lindy Hop class every Friday because I've paid for the next term in full. We have a date every week with cod and chips and a pickled egg. I am not going to just abandon her and go back to London. It's not going to be easy. It's going to be grim. But fucking hell, isn't that just life?

"I'm staying Violet" I tell her, "Don't try and argue with me."

"Alright then, stay. But you have to promise me if I start making a fool of myself you put me in a home and get on with your life. I'd like you to promise me you won't just settle. You must do what makes you happy, but not what makes you feel safe. There's a difference."

I cant believe this woman's mind is going to disappear. Life is so unfair.

She lifts my chin up and looks into my eyes, and says,

"Fish and chips?"

"Go on then. But you can't have them on Friday if we have them today. I mean that's twice in a–"

"Oh yes I can. The essential fatty oils in fish are very good for the brain and can help prevent–"

Oh here we go. Strap in.

***

[16]

It's about 5am, and I've woken up from a dream where I was lying on the beach, right on the shoreline, being thrown about by the waves like a doll. The sky is just getting lighter outside and it's strangely cold. I get up to grab a jumper, and hear something banging downstairs. I just have a weird feeling about it, so – I creep down, and the front door is swinging open and banging into the doorframe. Fuck. Fuck fuck fuck.

I grab a torch, and leave the house. Amazing what thoughts can go through your head in a situation like that. She's walked off the cliff top, is my main worry, she's been kidnapped – unlikely, but seems viable at 5am. Anything could have happened to her. It's almost automatic, going down to the beach. And that's where I find her. The light is barely there, and she looks like a ghost, stood right where the waves break, staring out to sea. She has absolutely no clothes on, and she's chatting away to the water, moving her body like an eighty-something water nymph. I'm not going to lie – it isn't a pretty sight. Her skin is so white and pale and I watch her for a while. Not in a creepy way, but – I don't know. Maybe it sounds silly but in that moment I just have *infinite* respect for her. I remember her photographs, what she said about her body. All she's doing here is standing naked on the beach. Zero shits given. People would say otherwise but I think there's dignity in that.

I don't want to frighten her, so I take off my jumper, and walk up to her slowly.

"What are you doing Violet?" I place the jumper gently around her shoulders and she smiles.

"Dancing" she says. She takes my hands in hers, and the jumper falls down onto the sand and is immediately licked by the sea. Fucking hell. Now she's starkers and we're both cold.

She starts moving my arms slowly, side to side.

"Dancing" she says again.

So I join in. Because that's what I've learned. That's what she's taught me. Don't worry about fixing it, finishing it. Don't try and run away. Just go with it. So Violet and I dance on the beach that morning, both of us crackers, and both of us free, and after a while, we make our way back to the house, now – I'd given her my pyjama top to pop on, so now I'm topless, clutching a damp jumper across my chest, and she has no pants on and a pyjama top that's too small. What a fucking sight. We get home and we warm her up.

And that's how it is. Some days she's angry
and gets naked at deeply inappropriate
moments, and some days we have tea
and play cards and go fishing and talk.
Unpredictable, chaotic. Just like everything
else.

***

[17]

It was my idea, to have another fire, and
I have to say for an old woman losing her
mind she's done a pretty impressive job at
building it.

The fire crackles and pops as a log splits–

"Violet – careful there's an ember on your
leg. Vi. Violet!"

She's just staring at the singed hole
that's formed in the blanket on her lap.
Like a kid looking at – I don't know – a
grasshopper.

What will happen from here? You know? I wonder how long it will take before it steals away who she is entirely. I hate the fact that her body will remain the same. I don't know if I can be there for all of it. If I'm brave enough to watch. I think about how stoic she's being and wonder if I should be stronger like she is. Less... Emotional.

Like, so earlier today we were sunbathing.

And, as we're sat there, she just – out of the blue just turns to me and says that as things worsen it's likely that she will start losing inhibitions. Start behaving in socially inappropriate ways. Yeah no shit Sherlock. Clearly she has no memory of our 5am naked dancing fandango. This is happening more and more actually – I know stuff about her that she doesn't. What a strange position to be in.

She turned to me again and said, "I'm telling you. My tits were incredible. Back in the day. It's a crying shame I can't get them out right now."

So I said, "Violet. What was it you were just saying about those inhibitions going?"

And we both laughed, and didn't mention it again all day. Sometimes – I think, maybe…

Sometimes unspoken is better actually.

Sometimes I think you can say more, when you just talk about… Tits.

***

The fire is dying down a bit now and she's stopped stoking it up. She's just lying back and looking at the sky. She's very still.

Jesus, she'd better not have fucking died on me.

No. She's… stargazing.

She points upwards to a constellation. "See that one? Well that's the Great Bear. Ursa Major, there's a story that goes with it…"

She tells me the story of The Great Bear
most nights. And every night I pretend it's
the first time I've heard it. But it doesn't
matter does it? I don't think it matters
that she'll forget any of it– youths spent in
Japan, lost baby boys, Lindy Hop classes,
lovers taking classy nudes, or that time near
the end of her life when she brought some
purpose to a very lost 27-year-old with a
penchant for pickled eggs. It happened, it
was lived, and all that matters is that those
stories were heard by someone.

All that really matters in the end, is that
someone listened.

WWW.OBERONBOOKS.COM